한 점에서 시작해
끝없이 커질 동그라미를
그려가는 길에
동행하게 되어
반갑고 기쁩니다
끝도없고 시작만 있을
불후의 짐도를
함께 축하 합시다

2025년 4월

제자
이원로 드림

Lee Won-Ro's 59th Poetry Collection

이원로 59번째 시집

The Sower

씨 뿌리는 사람

시산맥 기획시선　146

The Sower
씨 뿌리는 사람

시산맥 기획시선 146

초판 1쇄 인쇄 | 2025년 4월 28일
초판 1쇄 발행 | 2025년 5월 1일

지은이 이원로
펴낸이 문정영
펴낸곳 시산맥사
편집주간 김필영
편집위원 최연수 박민서
등록번호 제300-2013-12호
등록일자 2009년 4월 15일
주소 03131 서울특별시 종로구 율곡로6길 36. 월드오피스텔 1102호
전화 02-764-8722, 010-8894-8722
전자우편 poemmtss@naver.com
시산맥카페 http://cafe.daum.net/poemmtss

ISBN 979-11-6243-575-5 (03810) 종이책
ISBN 979-11-6243-576-2 (05810) 전자책

값 12,000원

* 이 책은 전부 또는 일부 내용을 재사용하려면 반드시 저작권자와 시산맥사의 동의를 받아야 합니다.
* 이 책은 교보문고와 연계하여 전자북으로 발간되었습니다.
* 본문 페이지에서 한 연이 첫 번째 행에서 시작될 때에는 〈 표기를 합니다.
* 저자의 의도에 따라 작품의 보조 동사와 합성 명사는 띄어쓰기가 달라질 수 있습니다.

Lee Won-Ro's 59th Poetry Collection
이원로 59번째 시집

The Sower
씨 뿌리는 사람

Lee Won-Ro 이원로

| Prologue |

Cross Section

Let us watch the flowing water,
It won't fight against obstacles
But will embrace and caress them as it passes,
Growing intimate over long years.

The towering rocky mountain
Where springs begin
Turns to pebbles along the riverbank,
And finally to grains of sand by the shore.

The flow of time
Will reveal all;
A stage of triumph and defeat-
A cross-section of a fleeting moment.

단면도

흐르는 물을 지켜보자
걸림돌과 싸우지 않으리
보듬어 쓰다듬으며 지나리
오랜 세월 친밀해져 가리

샘물이 시작되는
우람한 바위산이
강가의 자갈로 변하고
바닷가 모래알이 되지

시간의 흐름이
모두를 드러내리
이기고 지는 경연장
찰나의 단면도이지

■ 차 례

Part I Flower Rain
제1부 꽃비

A Cry of Admiration 경탄성	19
Arrow 화살	21
Freedom 자유	22
Flower Rain 꽃비	25
Dazzling Smile 황홀한 미소	27
Endless Game 연속 게임	29
Explore 탐험가	31
Permission 허락	33
Inseparable 불가분	35
The Comforter 위로자	37
Art and Science 예술과 과학	39

Part II The Sower
제2부 씨 뿌리는 사람

Strategy 책략	43
Reckless Expectations 무모한 기대	45
Abyss 구렁텅이	47
Eating and Living 먹고살기	49
Proof 입증	51
Round Dance 윤무	53
The Sower 씨 뿌리는 사람	55
Despair 절망	57
Dancing Together 함께 춤추지	59
Battery 배터리	61
Prayer 기도	63

Part III The River of Transformation
제3부 변환의 강

River of Transformation 변환의 강	67
Tears 눈물	69
The Day of Discontent 불만의 날	71
Unknown Soldier 무명용사	73
Fireworks 불꽃놀이	75
The Checkerboard and the Equation 바둑판과 방정식	77
Loss 손실	79
Rays of Light 빛살	81
Deep Bow 큰절	83
A Great Gap 큰 간격	85
The Trailhead 초입	87

Part IV Friend
제4부 친구

Circuits 회로	91
The Roots of Desire 소망의 뿌리	93
The Vast Ocean 망망대해	95
Nightmare 악몽	97
Mastery 통달	99
Friend 친구	101
Autumn Leaves 가을 잎사귀	103
Hunger and Thirst 허기와 갈증	105
Shedding 허물	107
Subconscious 잠재의식	109
Paradise 낙원	111

Part V Cave Paintings
제5부 동굴 벽화

Sky Plains 하늘 평원	115
Sunset 낙조	117
Early Spring 초봄	119
Mission 사명	121
Footsteps 발길	123
Transition 전환기	125
Prosperity 형통	127
Scars 흉터	129
Sustenance 양식	131
Clumsy Wisdom 어설픈 지성	133
Cave Paintings 동굴 벽화	135

Part I
Flower Rain

제1부
꽃비

A Cry of Admiration

Along the sunlit path,
flowering trees bloom brightly,
stretching their arms to touch the sky.

Yesterday, it was a shower of rain;
today, a shower of light.
The air is thick with awe.

The rays of light and drops of rain,
each boast of their own deeds,
wearing a triumphant smile.

The birds, in their own way,
believe the spectacle is for them,
soaring upward in admiration.

The sense of wonder deepens and lingers.
Something stirs from within,
as the earth and sky are docking together.

경탄성

빛살 내리는 산책길에
활짝 피어오르는 꽃나무들
온 팔을 뻗어 하늘에 닿았다

어제는 물세례로
오늘은 빛세례로
경탄성이 자욱하다

빛살과 빗발은 저 나름
공적을 미음에 뽐내며
회심의 미소를 짓는다

새들은 모두 저 나름
저를 위한 향연이라고
감탄하며 활개쳐 오른다

경탄성이 깊고 길어진다
안에서 무언가 툭 친다
하늘에 땅이 도킹 중이다

Arrow

Your time
May seem like it's yours,
But you know it's not, really.

An arrow shot forth,
Depending on aim and wind speed,
May hit the mark,
Or miss entirely.

An incoming arrow,
Casting a shadow of threat,
Or a flash of relief,
Alternating by the second.

Where and when you stand,
Will determine
Whether you laugh or cry.

화살

너의 시간은
네 것인 듯 실은
아닌 걸 알고 있지

쏘아대는 화살
조준과 풍속 따라
명중될 수도
빗나갈 수도 있으리

날아드는 화살
위협의 그림자
안도의 빛
분초로 교차하리

어느 때 어느 곳에
서게 되느냐로
웃기도 울기도 하리

Freedom

The boundless ocean calls out,
And I rush to ride the waves of freedom.

How can I endure the countless hours
Of solitary darkness?
How will I overcome the loneliness and despair
That surge relentlessly?

　I will plead in endless tears,
"Just don't let me lose hope."
I will cling, begging to return home,
To live in the peace of everyday life.

But even before the nightmare fades,
My heart, running along parallel lines,
Always crosses over, longing and dreaming.
I will be drawn back to the vast ocean.

Caught by an unyielding desire,
I risk my life to chase freedom.

자유

망망대해가 불러대니
자유를 타러 달려간다

홀로 맞는 헤아릴 수 없는
칠흑의 시간을 어찌 감당하지
시시각각 밀어닥치는
외로움과 절망을 이겨내려나

희망만 잃지 않게 해달라
한없이 눈물로 호소하리
집에 가 일상의 평안 속에
살게 해달라 매달리게 되리

그러나 악몽이 가시기도 전에
늘 건너가 그리워 꿈꾸는
평행선을 달리는 마음
다시 망망대해로 끌려 나가리

뿌리칠 수 없는 열망에 잡혀
목숨을 걸고 자유를 쫓아 가지

Flower Rain

Eyes silently fixed on
The pouring flower rain,
What stirs in the heart,
What breeze rises in the mind?

Is it the sound of a sigh,
Or the bitter waves of the setting sun?

Or perhaps, in the astonishing light,
The boundless dance of freedom riding waves?

In a face once filled with sighs,
Joy overflows.

Amidst the grand fireworks of a majestic finale,
Flowing and spreading forth,
The prelude to the shining season of harvest
Echoes with jubilation.

꽃비

쏟아져 내리는 꽃비를
묵묵히 응시하는 눈길
가슴엔 무엇이 꿈틀대지
머리엔 무슨 바람이 일지

탄식의 소리 들려오는가
해넘이의 쓸쓸한 물결인지

놀라운 빛 속에서 무한의
파도를 타는 자유의 춤인지

한숨짓던 얼굴에
희열이 가득 차 오네

장엄한 대단원의 불꽃놀이
가운데서 흘러 퍼져 내리는
열려올 빛나는 추수 계절의
환희의 전주곡을 들었으리

Dazzling Smile

In the corner of a valley,
A clumsy path,
I passed by without a glance,
Paying it no mind.

Who would have thought that
Such a humble door could be the entrance
To such a wondrous realm?

Intricate order,
Revelatory inspiration,
An endless unfolding-
Will I soon meet its master?

What clings to your thoughts,
What keeps drawing your heart,
Is the touch of an invitation.

If you couldn't handle it,
He wouldn't have invited you.
His dazzling smile
Awaits you there.

황홀한 미소

골짜기 구석
어설픈 길이기에
눈도 주지 않고
지나쳐 버렸다

보잘것없는 문이
이처럼 놀라운
나라의 입구라니

정교한 질서
계시적 영감의
끝없는 열림
곧 주인을 만날 건가

생각에 달라붙는 것
마음을 자꾸 끄는 건
초대의 손길이란다

감당치 못할 거면
그가 초대 안 했으리
그의 황홀한 미소가
거기서 기다리리

Endless Game

The whole world
Is a stage for an endless game
That cannot be stopped.

Action and reaction
Turn like gears,
Spinning without rest.

In an irrational world,
A rational approach will eventually
Elicit a subtle response.

Can the impulse of curiosity
Truly be persuaded
By the counsel of reason?

A procession of tension and anxiety
Trails through the straits
Of an iceberg in the fog.

Which path will you tread,
And where will you arrive?
It's a continuous game of give and take.

연속 게임

세상 모두는
멈출 수 없는
연속 게임의 무대

작용과 반작용이
톱니바퀴에 무려
그침 없이 돌지

비상식적 세상에서
상식적 접근은 결국
미묘한 반응을 낳으리

호기심의 충동이
지성적 조언으로
진정 설득되겠는지

긴장과 불안의 행렬이
안개 속 빙산의 해협을
꼬리를 물고 지나가리

어느 길을 밟아가며
어디에 도달할 건지
받고 주는 연속 게임이지

Explorer

Moment by moment,
Each step we take,
A wondrous and astonishing
Space unfolds.

It has never existed before,
And will never be seen again,
An immeasurably precious
Work of art.

As engraved deeply in each of us,
We run toward the call,
Into a marvelously intricate
And sublime panorama.

So, you and I,
Everyone,
Are explorers,
Pioneers.

탐험가

순간순간 각자가
발 들여 놓을 때마다
절묘하고 기막힌
공간이 펼쳐진다

전에도 없었고
앞으로도 다시 못 볼
헤아릴 수 없이
귀중한 예술품이지
각자마다 깊이
새겨넣어 준 대로
부르는 소리를 향해
놀랍게 정교하고
숭고한 파노라마 안으로
날려 나가면 돼

그러니 너와 나
누구나 모두
탐험가이며
선구자이지

Permission

Who would grant permission
To build a house upon anger?
Who would applaud and welcome
A tower raised from greed?

The seeds of collapse
Are already sown within.

Who would permit a nation
To be founded on vengeance?
How long could a union bound by betrayal
Possibly endure?

The signs of ruin
Are already lurking inside.

허락

분노 위에 짓는 집을
누가 허락해 주랴
탐욕으로 올리는 탑을
누가 손뼉 쳐 환영하랴

이미 그 안에
붕괴의 씨가 심겼지

보복 위에 세우는 나라를
누가 허락해 주겠나
반역으로 결속된 연합이
얼마나 오래 버티겠나

벌써 파멸의 조짐이
그 안에 도사려 있지

Inseparable

Cries out to the sky,
Grievances and complaints to the earth-
Is it from not truly knowing?
From seeing and hearing it wrong?

The most important things
Are unseen and unheard,
Only the heart can speak with them.

Just as space and time are inseparable,
So too are sky and earth bound,
An inseparable fate,
Revealed since the dawn of time.

When signals falter amidst the chaos,
The call falls into confusion,
Leaving us to cry out and complain in sorrow.

불가분

하늘을 향한 울부짖음
땅에 대한 한과 투정
제대로 몰라 그리하는지
잘못 보고 듣고 그러는지

가장 중요한 것들은
안 보이고 안 들리기에
오직 마음으로 대화하지

시공간이 불가분이듯
하늘과 땅도 결속된
불가분의 운명체인 걸
태초부터 보여주었지

교란에 신호가 흔들려
통화가 혼란에 빠지니
가엾게 울부짖고 투정하리

The Comforter

The conceited one,
Whose tangled mind plunged into chaos,
Mistook delusion for transcendence.

The foolish one,
Caught in hallucinations through sleepless night,
Swayed by excitement and fear.

How much longer must they wait?
What if it never comes?
Anxiously waiting, consumed with worry-

At last, restful sleep finds them,
Wrapped in peace,
For the Comforter is here.

The pitiful one,
Cradled in almighty arms,
Shall greet the joy of dawn.

위로자

우쭐한 자
뇌 망이 혼란에 빠져
망상을 초월로 착각했지

미련한 자
환각에 잡혀 밤새우며
흥분과 공포에 휘둘리지

얼마나 더 인가
안 오면 어찌할지
애태우며 기다리더니

이제야 단잠에 들었지
평화에 잠기었지
위로자가 함께해 서리

가련한 자
전능의 팔에 안기니
여명의 기쁨을 얻으리

Art and Science

Art and science,
Like the hemispheres of the brain,
Are complementary,
Not mutually exclusive.

Thus, in the world,
There is
No science without art,
And no art without science.

예술과 과학

예술과 과학은
두뇌의 반구처럼
서로 보완적이며
상호 배타적 아니지

그러니 세상엔
예술 없는 과학도
과학 없는 예술도
존재하지 않는다

Part II
The Sower

제2부
씨 뿌리는 사람

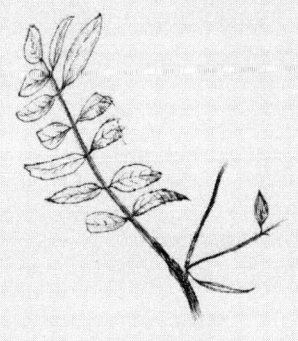

Strategy

Thinking the peak was near,
I grew complacent,
only to circle
the basecamp endlessly.

Believing I'd ventured deep,
I boasted, yet still flounder,
trapped in shallows,
thrashing aimlessly.

How far have I climbed
from those infant days?
Where innocence fades,
only schemes take root.

Countless strategies lie in wait,
dormant within me.
Which will take control,
and where will it lead?

책략

산정이 지척인 줄로
얕보아 자만하더니
베이스캠프를
맴돌 뿐이네

깊이 들어선 줄로
뻐기더니 아직도
천박 속에서 뒹굴며
허우적거릴 뿐이네

젖 먹던 시절에서
얼마나 기어오른 건가
천진난만이 사라진 곳에
모략만 무성히 자라다

내 안에 도사린
무수한 책략
어느 게 패권을 쥐고
어디로 끌어갈 건가

Reckless Expectations

Reckless expectations
Only leave wounds.

How could one grasp
The passage of time and space?
May the soul not suffocate
From indiscriminate hopes.

All rivers and mountains
Are already unique in their own way.
If they have fulfilled their role,
That should be enough.

How could you measure
The path of the heavens
With the yardstick of the earth?

무모한 기대

무모한 기대
상처만 내지

시공의 운행을 어찌
손아귀에 넣으려나
무분별한 기대로
영혼이 질식 안 되길

모든 강과 산은
이미 각기 특이하지
제 몫을 다 했다면
그것으로 충분하리

땅의 잣대로 어찌
하늘길을 재려는지

Abyss

Struggling tirelessly
To escape the abyss
Of envy and greed.

Endlessly seeking a chance
Day and night, enduring hardship,
To break free from the prison
Of distrust and betrayal.

How will you face the gravitational waves?
Will you truly race against light?
You only need to take the outstretched hand,
And together, you will run with boundless joy.

The hand of omnipotence
That casts out the forces of darkness
Will lift you up,
And you will enjoy freedom
In the midst of the marvelous light.

구렁텅이

시기와 탐욕의
구렁텅이에서
헤어 나오려
무던히 애쓰지

불신과 반역의
유형지를 벗어나려
밤낮으로 와신상담
기회를 엿보는 중이리

중력파와 어찌 마주 서려나
빛과 진정 경주를 벌이려나
다만 내민 손을 잡으면 돼
무한의 희열로 함께 달려가리

어둠의 세력을 내치는
전능의 손이 끌어 올려주리
놀라운 빛 가운데
자유를 누리게 되리

Eating and Living

Do you need to know it all to eat?
Do you analyze and confirm every sip?
If you trust what you see and hear,
then relax, eat, and drink with ease.

Who can know the whole world?
We don't understand all its wonders,
not even the depths of our own children,
nor ourselves, as we live our entire lives.

In the end, life is about making a living-
eating right, living right.
When you trust in your heart,
you can live and eat without doubt.

We eat to live, and live to eat,
unknowingly consuming, unknowingly living.
As life provides us with sustenance,
we eat, and we live, just as it comes.

먹고살기

내용을 다 알아야 먹니
분석해 확인 후 마시니
믿음이 가니 보고들은 대로
마음 놓고 먹고 마셔

누가 세상을 다 알리
놀라운 이치 다 모르지
제가 낳은 자식도 그 속 모르지
저도 모르며 평생 살지

세상만사 먹고 살기지
제대로 먹고 제대로 살기지
마음에 믿음이 가니
의심 없이 먹고살리

살려고 먹고 먹으려고 사니
모르며 먹고 모르며 사니
먹고살게 넣어준 대로
그렇게 먹고 그렇게 살아

Proof

In a world of proof,
lacking confidence,
we try endlessly
to prove ourselves.

When the reason for being is full,
there's no need to prove,
no need to display ourselves.

Earthly proof is temporary,
requiring endless repetition.
Heavenly proof is eternal,
fulfilling once and lasting forever.

입증

입증의 세상
자신감이 없기에
자신을 내보이려
끝없이 입증하리

존재 이유가 충만하면
저를 드러내려
입증할 이유 없으리

땅의 입증은 임시
한없이 반복해야지
하늘의 입증은 영구
단번에 충만 영속되리

Round Dance

The puller and the pulled meet,
gathering to dance in a circle.
Here and there intertwine,
joining and parting in turn.

The strength that uplifts the mind,
Offers a flag to wave.
The pull that stirs the heart,
Raises a kite high into the sky.

Each is an example to all,
Whether kind or cruel,
Great or small, strong or weak-
etching the patterns of the world as they go.

원무

끌기와 끌림이 만나
함께 모여 원무를 추지
거기와 여기가 얽히며
합쳐지고 갈라지게 되리

머리를 북돋는 힘이
흔들 깃발을 안겨주리
가슴을 울리는 끌림이
높이 연을 띄워 올리지

각자는 모두의 본보기
선량하건 악독하건
크건 작건 쎄건 약하건
세상 무늬를 새겨가지

The Sower

In the harsh cold of winter,
The one sowing seeds-
How could sprouts emerge?
When would flowers bloom?

Perhaps the sower misjudged
The passage of time,
Or get lost in distraction,
Now scrambling, in haste.

Sowing seeds is for all seasons,
Why, or for what reason?
There is no other way;
A mission, a quest, without doubt.

Through voice and images,
With all his heart and soul-
Alone in the wilderness,
The sower scatters seeds.

씨 뿌리는 사람

엄동설한에
씨 뿌리는 이
어찌 싹이 트라고
언제 꽃이 피라고

시간의 흐름을
잘 못 짚었는지
딴전 부리다가
허둥지둥하는지

씨 뿌리는 일은
사시사철이란다
왜인지 어째서인지
안 그러면 못 배긴단다

소리로 그림으로
마음과 심령 다해
광야에서 홀로
씨 뿌리는 사람

Despair

The greatest despair
is despair in oneself—
a false prophet, hoarding
the world's suffering.

At its core,
conceit lies hidden.

Fear and pain
rise from within,
masked so cunningly
that I deceive even myself.

Swept by dust-laden winds,
my mind's network falls into disarray.

Am I veering off course?
Circuits disrupted,
errors abound,
lost in a dark cloud.

Despair is but an illusion,
a delusion born of indoctrination.

절망

가장 큰 절망은
저에 대한 절망
세상 고뇌를 독차지한
거짓 선지자 모습

그 밑바닥엔
오만이 도사려 있지

두렵고 아픈 건
제 안에서 나오지
변장술이 교활해
저도 속으며 살아

먼지바람에 휩쓸려
뇌 망이 교란에 삐지리

궤도를 이탈하려느냐
회로에 교란이 일고
접속 오류가 난무하리
암운 속에 길을 잃으리

절망은 허상에
세뇌된 착각이지

Dancing Together

On the same stage,
Yet the eyes see,
The ears hear,
Each in their own way.

Perspectives shift,
focus changes,
clarity wavers,
as the self intercedes.

We may cry together, but for different reasons,
dance together, yet to different melodies,
receive together, yet in different measure and kind-
perhaps following an unseen intent.

함께 춤추지

같은 무대인데
눈 따라
귀 따라
천차만별

시각이 달라지지
집중도가 변하리
해상력이 출렁이지
자아 개입에 따라

같이 우는데 동기가 다르지
함께 춤추나 선율이 다르지
더불어 받으나 질과 양이 다르지
숨은 이의 의도를 따라선가

Battery

As the light flickers and fades,
Monsters and grotesques take the stage.
Even knowing they're fake, your heart still trembles.
wandering for survival until the nightmare breaks.

With a weak battery,
it barely holds on and easily cuts off,
staying connected for hours but never fully charging,
sometimes catching fire from overcharging.

Why lock away the built-in battery,
The one that charges well in the light,
deep inside the closet,
While staking our lives on an artificial one?

배터리

빛이 가물가물 꺼져가니
괴물과 흉물이 무대를 연다
가짜인 줄 알면서도 가슴 떨리지
살길 찾아 헤매다가 흉몽을 깬다

배터리가 시원치 않으니
겨우 버티다가 쉽게 끊어지리
오래 접속해도 충전 안 되리
과충전으로 불나기도 하지

빛만 들면 잘 충전시킬
붙박이 배터리는 어찌
벽장 속에 깊이 잠가두고
인조 배터리에 목숨을 거는가

Prayer

An urgent cry rings out-
is it facing danger,
or deep in pain?

A sharp caw echoes
through the entire forest.

Every sound, glance, and movement
is nothing but prayer,
a yearning, a plea, a cry for help.

Is it sending signals
on the right frequency?

All it knows is only this,
and it has nothing else to give,
so it offers all it has in full.

기도

심상치 않은 외침
위험에 직면했는지
심히 아파서인지

깍깍 울부짖는 소리
온 숲에 울려 퍼진다

소리 눈길 몸짓 모두
기도 아닌 게 없으리
 갈망 간구 호소이지

주파수가 맞는 신호를
보내고는 있는 건지

아는 게 고작 그게 다지
그것밖에 가진 게 없으니
그렇게 다 바치는 거지

Part III
The River of Transformation

제3부
변환의 강

River of Transformation

The river of endless transformation-
Crossing border upon border,
Winding and stretching across the continents,
A grand lifeline reaching the ocean.
Along every path, it blossoms, bearing fruit,
A river of life formed through transformation.

In droughts that lay bare the riverbed,
In trials too heavy to endure,
Barely after the cheers for rain subside,
Threatening floods come surging forth.
Brushing past endless clashes and crises,
It will finally reach its destined sea.

A turning point comes in moments of deep inspiration;
Transformation grows through peril and hardship,
Maturing under the weight of oppression and trials.
The river of transformation fulfills its purpose,
Crossing the sea to touch the sky,
It shall bear witness to all the insight gained along the great journey.

변환의 강

그침 없는 변환의 강-
국경의 고비를 넘고 또 넘어
굽이굽이 대륙을 횡단하지
바다에 이르는 장관의 삶 줄
길마다 꽃 피워 열매를 맺지
변환으로 이루는 생명의 강-

바닥이 드러나는 가뭄
감당 못 할 고뇌와 고난
단비의 환호가 식기도 전
위협적 홍수가 밀려오지
무한한 충돌과 위기를 스쳐
대망의 바다에 이르게 되리

전환의 계기는 큰 감동의 순간
위난과 고초로 변환은 자라고
핍박과 탄압으로 여물어 가지
변환의 강은 소임을 다하는 삶 줄
바다를 건너서 하늘에 닿으리
장도의 견문을 모두 증언하리

Tears

Our history is
The trail of tears.

Tears of meeting and parting,
Of victory and defeat,
Of regret and confession,
Of gratitude and resentment.

As countless as stars in the sky,
As varied as the grass and flowers of the earth,
So are the tears we shed.

Tears are the wellspring of truth
Rising from the core of deep emotion.

Tears are the door to truth,
The door to new hope,
The priming water for joy,
A gateway into a new world.

According to the source of inspiration,
And the purity of the tears,
The intensity of their resonance arises.

눈물

우리의 역사는
눈물의 행적

만남과 이별
승리와 패배
후회와 고백
감사와 원망의 눈물

하늘의 별만큼이나
땅의 풀과 꽃처럼
무수하고 다양하리

눈물은 감동의 중추에서
솟아오르는 진실의 샘물

눈물은 진리의 문
새 소망의 문
기쁨의 마중물
새 나라로 드는 문

감동의 원천에 따라
눈물의 순도에 따라
울림의 강도가 생기지

The Day of Discontent

The day I longed for so deeply,
That once seemed it might someday come,
Now unfolds before me.

In awe of this astonishingly beautiful day,
What thoughts arise within me?
What emotions stir inside you?
What are you doing,
And how am I spending this moment?
Are such thoughts and feelings,
In truth, too undeserved a gift to receive?

The day of discontent
Lies not in that day itself,
But rather within the discontent.

불만의 날

그토록 소망하던
언젠간 올 것 같던
그런 날이 펼쳐진다

놀랍게 아름다운
그날을 맞이하여
어떤 생각에 잠기지
무슨 마음이 꿈틀대지
너는 무얼하고 있어
나는 어찌하고 있지
그런 마음과 생각이
내려받기에는 실로
과분한 선물은 아닌지

불만의 날은
그날에 있지 않고
그 불만에 있지

Unknown Soldier

Unseen,
Unheard,
Forgotten things
Nurture and guide the world.

Deeply cherished hopes,
Patient, enduring prayers,
Faith that does not waver
Through rain, snow,
Or fierce winds -
The driving force of progress.

Someone will stand alongside,
There will be one to guard,
Planting in the heart of the unknown soldier
A fire that sparks miracles.

무명용사

안 보이고
안 들리는
잊힌 것들이
세상을 키우고
이끌어 가리

깊이 간직한 소망
참고 기다리는 간구
비가 오고 눈이 와도
바람이 불어도
흔들리지 않는 믿음
바퀴의 원동력이지

누군가 함께하리
지켜주는 이 있으리
무명용사의 심장에
기적을 일으키는
불을 심어주리

Fireworks

Our days are
A festival of change,
Stirring the heart.

What kind of scenario
Will adorn
The final common path
We all must tread?

Will it be bold,
Despairing,
Or thrilling?

Why keep worrying,
Agonizing over something
Already decided?

It will be
A once-in-a-lifetime
Display of fireworks,
Awe-inspiring and heart-lifting.

불꽃놀이

우리의 나날은
마음을 흔드는
변화의 축제

누구나 밟게 될
최종 공동통로를
어떤 시나리오가
장식해 줄 건가

담대할지
낙담할지
전율할지

이미 결정된 걸
언제까지
고심하며
마음 졸이려나

평생에 한 번 있을
놀라워 가슴 부풀
불꽃놀이일 거야

The Checkerboard and the Equation

The world is a checkerboard:

An intricate weave,
A marvel of planning and precision-
A structure that seems dry and repetitive,
A melody that feels monotonous ans tedious,
Yet it holds every breath and heartbeat
Of body and mind, thought and soul.
You can see the gestures of genes,
Hear the whispers of cells.

The universe is an equation:

The densest poetry of the cosmos,
A banner of astonishing order and power-
A seemingly dry array of symbols and numbers,
A code that feels bored and complex,
And yet, hidden within, are the breaths and Rhythms of
the macro and microcosm.
Galaxies and constellations lay bare their hearts,
And the rushing waves of the Big Bang can be felt.

바둑판과 방정식

세상은 바둑판:

정교한 짜임새
놀라운 계획과 능력이지
무미건조 반복의 구조인 듯
천편일률 지루한 선율인 듯
몸과 마음 생각과 영혼의
모든 숨과 박동이 담겨 있지
유전자들의 몸짓이 보이리
세포들의 속삭임을 들으리

우주는 방정식:

가장 농축된 우주의 시어
놀라운 질서와 능력의 깃발이지
메마른 문자 숫자의 배열인 듯
지루하고 난해한 암호인 듯
대우주 미세우주의 모든
호흡과 율동이 여기 숨어 있지
은하와 성좌가 심장을 드러내 가지
쇄도하는 빅뱅의 물결이 느껴지리

Loss

It's just a fleeting dream,
So why, at its sudden loss,
Does it strike the heart so deeply?

I know that's how it is,
But knowing does not mean
The heart will comply.

How could one alone bear
The invisible world's
Countless entanglements?

The spirit tries to accept,
Thoughts scatter in confusion,
And feelings shatter the heart.

손실

본시 스쳐 가는 꿈인데
왜 졸지의 손실이라고
그처럼 가슴을 치는지

그런 줄은 알지만
그렇다고 그게 어찌
마음대로 되겠는지

볼 수 없는 세상의
헤아릴 수 없는 얽힘을
어찌 홀로 감당하겠는지

심령은 받아들이려 하리
생각은 허둥거리고
느낌은 가슴이 무너지지

Rays of Light

Lift your eyes and look,
Astonishing rays of light pouring
Through the branches and leaves,
Riding along the optic nerve,
Shaking the net of the brain.

In every shadowed valley,
Even in the dark pits within,
Rays of light will overflow.
The repugnant river in the heart,
Overflowing with filth,
Will be brilliantly cleansed.

Where there's metabolism,
Waste tends to accumulate.
The wondrous light of the sky
Pours down endlessly,
Burning it away without cease.

빛살

눈을 들어 바라보라
가지와 잎새 사이로
쏟아지는 놀라운 빛살
시신경을 타고 들어가
뇌 망을 흔들어 대리

그늘진 골짜기마다
암울한 구덩이 안에도
빛살이 넘쳐흐르리
구정물이 범람하는
가슴 안 역겨운 강도
빛나게 말끔히 세탁하리

신진대사 있는 곳엔
노폐물이 쌓여가지
경이로운 하늘빛이
끊임없이 쏟아내려
거침없이 살라버리지

Deep Bow

Climbing up to resolve
The piled-up curiosities,
They'll follow the path
Toward where the door may open.

Reaching the summit,
He kneels down,
Presses his forehead to the ground,
And offers a deep bow.

A world once unseen
Unfolds beneath his feet,
And suddenly, overcome with awe,
He humbly prostrates himself.

Are you, lost in grandeur,
Trying to steal that bow for yourself?
And why do I, hesitating,
Only glance around, self-conscious?

큰절

쌓여온 궁금증을
올라가 풀어보려
문이 열릴 쪽으로
제 길을 따라가리

정상에 오르더니
그는 무릎을 꿇고
머리를 땅에 묻고
큰절을 올리지

안 보이던 세상을
발아래 깔아주니
문득 경외심에 눌려
황공해 엎드렸으리

너는 호연지기에 빠져
그 절을 훔쳐 받으려느냐
나는 어찌 엉거주춤
주위 눈치만 살피는지

A Great Gap

A great gap,
Uncrossable,
Unattainable,
Seemingly far away-
And yet,

Human potential sometimes
Surpasses imagination,
Transcends the impossible;
An unconscious gift
Bestowed upon us.

For those who believe in miracles,
Mystery becomes everyday life.
What is your miracle?
Is there no miracle within you?
Are you not a miracle yourself?

큰 간격

큰 간격
건널 수 없는
이룰 수 없는
까마아득한 듯
하지만

인간의 능력은 때론
상상을 초월하지
불가능을 넘어서지
실은 저도 모르게
내려받은 권능이지

기적을 믿는 이에겐
신비가 일상이 되리
너의 기적은 어떤 건가
너에겐 기적이 없는지
너 자체가 기적 아닌지

The Trailhead

Knocking, seeking, searching-
What have you found,
Whom have you met?

Every meeting is just the beginning,
The journey's end is never truly the end.
This is the trailhead rising up,
The base camp of hope.

If the days of looking ahead
Are without end,
Could there be anything better?

초입

두드려 구하고 찾아
무엇을 얻었는지
누구를 만났는지

만남은 오직 시작
땅끝은 끝이 아니리
거기로 오르는 초입
기대의 베이스캠프

바라다보는 날이
끝이 없다면
더 좋은 게 또 있으랴

Part IV
Friend

제4부
친구

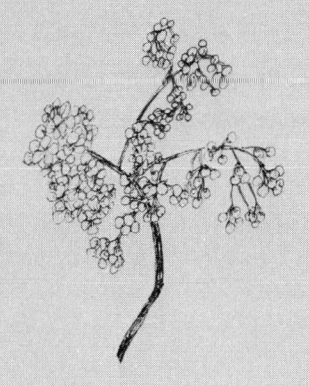

Circuits

At the brink of life and death,
All other circuits shut down,
And body and mind unite wholly
To secure a path to survival.

Those circuits of restraint and suppression,
So challenging in daily life,
Astonishingly engage in moments of crisis,
Pausing everything else
And mobilizing every channel to preserve life.

The root of crisis is the everyday;
Acuteness is the result of the chronic.
The central command is strong in emergencies,
Yet fragile in the routine of daily life.

회로

생사의 기로에선
딴 회로는 다 닫히고
활로를 확보하려
심신이 온통 집결하지

일상 그처럼 어렵던
억제와 차단의 회로가
위기일발을 만나니
놀랍게 이처럼 작동하지
모두를 일시 중단하고
살릴 회로를 총동원하리

위기의 근본은 일상
급성은 만성의 결과
응급에는 강한 중추
일상엔 취약한 관제탑

The Roots of Desire

How immense must the hatred be
To fulfill that desire for vengeance,
Willing even to sacrifice one's life
Just to achieve it.

How could this be?
Surely, they must have lost their senses.

How profound must the love be
To save you,
Willing to die in your place
Just to fulfill that hope.

How can this be?
Can this be done in one's right mind?

What are
The roots of desire?
Who is
The source of such sacrifice?

소망의 뿌리

얼마나 원한이 크기에
 그 원수를 갚을 수만 있다면
목숨을 바쳐서라도
 그 소망을 이루려 하지

어찌 이럴 수가
제정신을 잃었으리

얼마나 사랑이 깊기에
너를 살릴 수만 있다면
나를 대신 죽여서라도
그 소망을 이루려 하지

세상에 이럴 수가
제정신에 이러는 건가

소망의 뿌리는
무엇이지
희생의 원천은
누구지

The Vast Ocean

Living wrapped in a cozy embrace,
These peaceful days are nice enough,
Yet when restlessness and frustration grow,
I long to break away and journey far.

Surrounded by charming islands,
The view of the archipelago is lovely,
Yet I yearn for the boundless open sea,
Where nothing obstructs the endless horizon.

In the depths of our genes,
Etched from the beginning of time,
Is an inescapable path of destiny,
Like the wind, the clouds, the water.

Drawn by distant calls and gestures,
One day, in some unknown place,
To meet the one who waits,
I urge myself on this endless route.

Since the call never ceases,
I cannot stay in one place;
Following the course given to me,
I set forth as a traveler.

망망대해

포근한 품에 안겨 사는
아늑한 나날도 좋으련만
싫증 나고 답답해
떨치고 멀리 떠나가려나

아담한 섬들에 둘린
다도해의 풍광도 좋으련만
앞이 탁 터인 거칠 것 없는
망망대해가 그리워 서지

태초에 유전자 안에
깊숙이 새겨 넣어준
어쩔 수 없는 숙명의 행로
바람과 구름과 물처럼

손짓과 부름에 끌려
언젠가 알 수 없는 곳에서
기다리는 누군가를 만나러
끝없는 항로를 재촉하지

그침 없이 부르기에
한군데 못 머물리
주어진 항해도 따라
나그넷길을 떠나지

Nightmare

Trembling, grotesque, and terrifying,
Images of monsters, horrors, and demons-
Is there still more left to create?

Though the costumes and makeup may differ,
No matter how deeply I try to portray them,
No new forms will come to mind.

An advanced scientist, a man of intellect,
Yet all night long, haunted and crushed
By the monsters and demons of my own making.

Am I still living in the grip of darkness?
Is there fear both inside and out?
The nightmare is my brain's self-portrait on display.

Living with my back turned to the light,
Caught in the path of hollow illusions,
Struggling, lost in the swamp of nightmares.

악몽

떨리고 징그럽고 무서운
괴물 흉물 악귀 이미지들
아직도 그릴 게 더 남았는지

의상과 화장만 다를 뿐
마음과 혼을 다해 그리려 해도
더는 새 모습 안 떠오르리

첨단 과학자 지성인인데
제가 만든 흉물 괴물 악귀에
밤새껏 짓눌리고 시달리리

아직 어둠에 잡혀 사는지
안과 밖이 모두 두려운지
악몽은 뇌 망에 전시된 자화상

빛을 등지고 살기에
가짜 홀림 길에 빠져
악몽의 늪에서 허덕이지

Mastery

It won't be easy to master,
Even after enduring endless trials,
How could it ever be guaranteed?

Though you seek and are lifted up,
Tumbling back and forth,
Rising and falling-
An endless staircase,
With an unpredictable course,
Destination unknown.
Still, everyone longs
To arrive there someday.

Starting is half the journey,
A lifelong struggle,
A birthright ailment.

통달

통달하기 쉽지 않으리
천신만고를 겪는다고
어찌 보장될 일인가요

구하고 끌어주어도
엎치락뒤치락
오르락내리락
끝없는 계단
어디에 이를지
예측 불가의 항로
그래도 누구나
그리되고 싶으리

시각이 반이지
평생 씨름할
배냇병이지

Friend

Wherever you go,
You will encounter a friend.
Even if you don't realize it,
A companion is already waiting for you.

In a heart trembling with fear,
A new meeting brings new hope.
From the friend who waits you,
You will gain new strength.

A destined encounter,
A waiting prepared-
An ordinary friend, it seems,
Yet one extraordinary.

Before you cry out,
Before you know it,
A friend to work beside you
Is already there, waiting.

We are all companions,
Friends meeting and waiting.
Who are you to me?
And who am I to you?

친구

언제 어디를 가도
친구를 만나게 되리
못 알아차려도 이미
기다리는 동행자이지

두려워 떠는 마음에
새 만남은 새 희망
기다리는 친구에게서
새 힘을 받게 되리

예정된 만남
준비된 기다림
예사 친구인 듯
특별한 친구지

울부짖기 전
모르는 사이
이미 함께 일할
친구가 기다리지

우리는 모두 동행자
만나고 기다리는 친구
너는 나의 누구지
나는 너의 누구인지

Autumn Leaves

Beneath the vast, blue sky,
On branches swaying endlessly,
Leaves dance with a surprising grace.

A trembling motion of fear,
A bold counterattack lunging forward-
But surely, it's not like that.

Autumn leaves are somehow different,
Perhaps it's the unique autumn breeze
That makes them dance this way.

The coming winter is unstoppable,
Rather than reckless battles, it's a wise truce,
Rehearsing gentle steps to cross over warmly.

Autumn leaves are somehow different,
They learn the steps to embrace the future,
It's a graceful dance of wise victory.

가을 잎사귀

드높고 푸른 하늘 아래
쉼 없이 흔들리는 가지에
놀랍게 춤추는 잎사귀들

두려워 떠는 몸짓
달려드는 당찬 반격
분명 그러진 않아

가을 잎새는 무언가 달라
무언가 나른 가을바람이
이렇게 춤추게 해주나 봐

다가올 겨울은 아무도 못 막으리
무모한 대결보단 지혜로운 하해지
포근히 넘을 스텝을 리허설 중이리

가을 잎사귀는 무언가 달라
미래를 품을 발짝을 익혀가지
슬기롭게 이길 춤곡 스텝이지

Hunger and Thirst

In a poor heart
With nothing to lose,
Hunger and thirst
Write and carve,
Singing and dancing.

Above the horizon,
Within the waves,
The hidden eternity
Is uncovered and revealed,
Shown with resolute strength.

Only the hunger and thirst
Of a humble soul
Can see the land of longing
Wherever the gaze reaches,
Amid the movement of fingertips.

허기와 갈증

가난한 마음의
잃을 것 없는
허기와 갈증을
쓰며 그리고 새겨
노래하며 춤추리

수평선 위에
물결 안에
숨겨둔 영원을
들추어 드러내
의연히 보여주리

가난한 영혼의
허기와 갈증만이
눈길이 닿는 곳에
손가락 놀림 가운데
동경의 나라를 보리

Shedding

How could this
dazzling and beautiful
forest of paradise
turn into a stage for slaughter?

Nowhere in this world
Will you find a place without snakes;
Even in Eden,
the serpent roamed freely.

Its disguise is so cunning,
A world that doesn't even recognize itself.
The more it sheds its skin,
the more wicked the serpent becomes.

허물

어찌 이처럼
눈부시고 아름다운
낙원의 숲이
살육의 무대가 되지

세상 어디에도
뱀이 없는 데는 없으리
에덴동산에서도
뱀이 누비고 다녔어

변장술이 너무 놀라워
저도 저를 몰라보는 세상
허물을 벗어 던질수록
뱀은 더 악독해 지지

Subconscious

The patterns of the world
Are perceived and stored
Even beyond conscious thought-
Such is the incredible realm of the subconscious.

Through subtle circuits
And hidden synapses,
It slips into the realm of awareness,
Secretly stirring the neural pathways.

Layered over generations,
Patterns quietly accumulated over time
Lie deep within the subconscious,
Ruling the foundations of consciousness.

잠재의식

세상 사물의 패턴은
생각 못 하는 사이에도
인식되고 저장되리
잠재의식의 놀라운 영역이지

감지되지 않는 오묘한
회로와 시냅스를 동원해
의식 영역을 비집고 들어와
은밀히 신경망을 흔들지

세대와 세대를 거치며
오랜 세월 모르게 쌓인
잠재의식 안 패턴들이
의식의 근저를 지배하지

Paradise

The sea is a vast pond,
Nothing but an aquarium-
With palms and white sands,
Fish and coral reefs.

A land of sun and waves,
An eternal Arcadia.

Mother says she wants
To live here forever,
But her daughter grew tired of paradise
And left for the digital world.

Even as sharks swarm,
The dolphins keep dancing.

낙원

바다는 큰 연못
다름 아닌 수족관
야자와 백사장
물고기와 산호초

태양과 파도의 나라
영원한 도원경

엄마는 언제까지나
여기서 살고 싶단디
딸은 낙원이 지겨워
디지털 세상으로 떠났지

상어가 들끓어도
돌고래는 춤추지

Part V
Cave Paintings

제5부
동굴 벽화

Sky Plains

An outdoor fitness ground,
A striking figure on the bench,
Lying flat, limbs outstretched,
Running with all fours raised to the sky.

Deeply immersed in the splendid autumn sky,
A triumphant smile ripples across.

Gaining speed, accelerating forward,
Limbs moving swiftly in rhythm,
A leopard races across the grasslands,
Its four legs sprinting over the sky plains.

Where is it headed, and for what purpose?
Perhaps to meet its master and grow wings.

하늘 평원

야외 심신 단련장
벤치 위에 눈 끄는 거동
반듯이 드러누워 사지를
하늘로 치켜세워 달리네

멋진 가을 하늘에 푹 빠져
회심의 미소가 물결친다

속력에 가속이 붙어 간다
쌀다리 리듬이 새빠르다
표범이 초원을 가로지른다
네발이 하늘 평원을 질주한다

무얼 하러 어딜 가는 건지
주인을 만나 날개를 달으려나

Sunset

Meeting in a remarkable era,
Crossing the sea to reunite,
On a rainy autumn morning,
A Zoom gathering of familiar old faces.

Their eyes sparkle brightly,
But there's no rush to speak.
This is not a stage for tales of valor,
Nor the age of fervent debates.
Referring to the harvest moon obscured by clouds,
Their eyes are drifting into a world of fairy tales.
A recent brush with death
Is dismissed with a casual smile.

With just the glances and expressions,
They are exploring each other's inner worlds,
Gazing quietly at the dazzling sunset over the sea,
They see each other's reflections.

낙조

놀라운 시대를 만나
바다를 넘어 만나지
가을장마 비 내리는 아침
옛 얼굴들의 줌 모임

눈빛은 영롱하지만
말을 서둘지 않으니
무용담 경쟁 무대는 아니리
열변의 토론 시대도 넘은 듯
한가위 날이 구름에 가렸다며
동화의 세계에 빠져 있는 눈
기사회생의 최근 위기를
예사인 듯 흘려버리는 미소

눈빛과 표정만으로 서로의
안 세상을 더듬어 보고 있으리
눈부신 낙조의 바다를 물끄러미
응시하는 서로의 모습들이지

Early Spring

One sunny early spring day,
by a brook swollen with passing spring rain,
a mother held a sprouting vine in one hand
and, with her soft other hand, clasped
the wrist of her young son, just barely recovered
from an illness that had nearly claimed him.

As she gazed endlessly into her child's eyes,
tears welled up in her own.
It was the first time he had seen his mother cry.
He didn't know why, but it carved itself deep in his heart.
Out front, carpenters were busy
preparing his great-grandmother's casket,
while in the courtyard, women's hands
worked tirelessly, sewing the burial shroud.

When green barley shoots covered the fields,
and vines stretched upward in early spring,
that boy, now graying and weathered,
would recall his mother's first tears.
Tears quietly fill his eyes, the same eyes his mother had
gazed so intently into back then.

초봄

화창한 이른 봄 어느 날
스쳐 간 봄비에 흐르는 도랑 가
돋아나는 덩굴을 한 손에 쥐고
엄마의 부드러운 다른 손은
구사일생 병을 털고 일어난
어린 아들의 손목을 쥐었지

아이의 눈을 하염없이 바라보는
엄마의 눈에 눈물이 고여들었지
아이가 처음 본 엄마의 눈물이지
왜인지 모르게 가슴 깊이 새겨졌지
앞뜰엔 증조모의 관을 준비하는
목수들의 작업이 한창이었고
안마당엔 수의를 지어가느라
아낙네들의 손길이 분주하였지

보리싹이 푸르게 앞 밭을 덮고
초봄의 덩굴이 뻗어 오르는 날이면
백발이 성성해진 그때 그 아이
엄마의 첫 눈물을 상기하지
엄마가 그때 뚫어지게 바라보던
그의 눈에 눈물이 하염없이 고여오지

Mission

What occupies your heart now,
Who holds it captive?

What governs your soul now,
Who is pulling the strings?

Heart and soul,
Like the wind, like the clouds,
You hope they will not waver.

Are you sure it's your mission,
Whose will is it?
What is it you pursue?

사명

지금 너의 마음
무엇이 차지하지
누구에게 잡혀 있지

지금 너의 영혼
무엇이 지배하지
누가 조종하지

마음과 영혼
바람같이 구름처럼
요동하지 않길 바라지

사명인 건 확실한지
누구의 뜻인지
무엇의 추구인지

Footsteps

A lonely flag flutters
in an empty sky,
an unnamed flower blooms alone
in a desolate field,
and aimless footsteps roam
through the deep universe.

There is a wind
That makes it flutter,
A touch
That planted it there,
A call
That lifted it to roam.

The day it catches the wind,
it will meet its owner.
The moment it sees the hand,
it will gain a name.
The instant it hears the call,
its way will open.

발길

빈 하늘에 퍼덕이는
임자 없는 깃발
황야에 홀로 핀
이름도 없는 꽃
심우주를 누비는
정처 없는 발길

펄럭이게 해주는
바람이 있지
거기에 심어준
손길이 있지
누비게 올려준
부름이 있지

바람을 잡는 날
임자를 만나리
손길을 보는 시간
이름을 얻게 되리
부름을 듣는 순간
갈 길이 열려오리

Transition

Early reeds glance around,
thinking summer has already passed,
drawn along by the fresh new breeze.

Trees in the hills and fields, too,
are bewildered by shifting light and wind,
wondering what colors will soon
cloak them, waiting in anticipation.

They shake off the lingering haze
of last night's fading dreams,
hoping soft, gentle hues
will soon warm their hearts and souls.

A time of transition is a world in disarray;
may each step be light and gentle,
and the path ahead smooth and clear.

전환기

여름이 이미 간 줄 알고
두리번대는 이른 갈대들
새바람에 끌려 따라왔으리

산과 들의 나무도 바뀌는
바람과 빛살에 어리둥절
어떤 옷을 입혀줄지
마음 졸이며 기대하리

어리벙벙한 어젯밤 꿈일랑
말끔하게 떨어 던져버리고
고운 빛깔이 마음과 혼을
포근히 품길 못 내 바라지

전환기는 어수선한 세상
내딛는 발걸음이 사뿐 가볍고
달려가는 길이 평탄하길 빌리

Prosperity

Though one may rely on a greater power,
anxiety and fear often arise
when stepping into the unfamiliar.

But this is no reason to lose heart-
one foot is already on the path,
and fear becomes a chance for renewed resolve.

In times of clinging to grace,
And wielding it like a servant,
It was used as a license for wrongdoing.

When trying to escape the den of lies,
Chaos and struggle inevitably ensue,
Until the moment for a turnaround is seized.

Prosperity is not mere complacency,
But a steadfast flow like a mighty river,
Surpassing fear, doubt, and inner turmoil.

형통

큰 힘에 늘 의지한다지만
낯선 곳에 들어가려면
불안과 두려움이 앞서리

그래도 의기소침은 아니니
이미 한 발은 올라선 거리
두렴은 실로 분발의 기회리

은혜를 붙들어서
종처럼 부리던 시절
악행의 면허로 삼았지

거짓의 소굴을 벗어나려니
혼란과 난투에 휘말리지
반전의 기회를 잡을 떼까지

형통이 무사안일은 아니지
불안과 의심과 고뇌를 넘는
의연한 장강의 흐름이지

Scars

The surface seems fine,
But inside, it's full of wounds-
scars inflicted from without,
and injuries caused from within.

Some are gained in cold wars,
some in battles of heat,
others appear in fits of anger,
or through a sarcastic sneer.

What was I pushing so hard to achieve,
driving myself to such extremes?
Was that how I survived,
even in the eye of the tornado?

Even if the wounds are shared,
scars will differ depending on their care-
they flash briefly in a passing gaze,
or reveal themselves mid-conversation.

흉터

겉은 멀쩡한데
속은 상처투성이
밖에서 받은 흉터
안이 저지른 상처

냉전 하다 받고
열전 하다 나지
심통 부려 입고
냉소 띠며 나지

무얼 이루려 그처럼
심하게 다그쳐 왔는지
토네이도 가운데서도
그래서 살아남았는지

큰 상처를 같이 받더라도
다스림 따라 흉터는 다르리
눈빛 가운데 흘깃 보이지
대화 도중 문득 드러나리

Sustenance

What you live on
Is who you are.
Roots may be inherited,
but the environment shapes you.

What you consume,
how you consume it,
and why you consume it,
will reveal your true nature.

How can exercise undo
the poison of alcohol, cigarettes, or drugs?
Can reckless indulgence
be cured by a simple tonic?

Your daily
sustenance
is the source
of your ultimate outcome.

양식

네가 먹고사는 게
네가 누구냐이지
근본은 타고나지만
환경이 너를 키우리

무얼 먹고사는지
어떻게 머고
왜 먹는지 따라
네 모습 드러나리

술 담배 마약의 독을
어찌 운동이 빼내 주리
마구잡이 배 채우기가
보야으로 해결될는지

매일의
양식이
최종결과의
원천이지

Clumsy Wisdom

How could a single rejection
Mean a permanent "no"?
A single refusal surely
Is not a lasting abandonment.

Overreactions are simply
disguised expressions of pride.

With plans and methods
beyond your grasp,
at the right time and place,
a good gift will come to you.

A closed door is a signal to take another path;
rejection is a gesture to wait.

Hold on to the thoughts of heaven,
not the thoughts of earth;
delight in the joy of heaven,
not in fleeting earthly pleasures.

Let not a clumsy wisdom
block the world beyond your understanding.

어설픈 지성

한번 퇴짜가 어찌
영원한 불가이겠나
한번 거절이 분명
영원한 버림은 아니리

과도한 반응은
자만의 표출이지

네 생각이 못 미치는
계획과 방법으로
시간과 장소를 골라
네게 좋은 선물을 주리

막는 건 돌아가라는 눈짓
불합격은 기다리라는 신호

땅의 생각이 아니라
하늘의 생각을 붙들란다
땅의 기쁨이 아니라
하늘의 기쁨을 즐기란다

파악 너머의 세계를
어설픈 지성이 가로막지

Cave Paintings

A group dwelling trapped in a cave,
longing for light, weary of darkness,
perhaps drawing the sun and moon on the walls.
By day, they hunt fiercely,
By night, they cry in sorrow.

On horseback, with bows and spears,
to fill their bellies, to claim more ground,
they hunt beasts and even hunt people,
relentlessly killing all they can.

Just as they bring down their prey,
in the final, gasping breaths,
they meet the indescribable gaze-
eyes that hold a mysterious world within.

The gaze embedded deep within the soul-
fearsome, yet awakening a longing for that distant realm.
Steadying their hearts, they paint on the cave walls,
whether of worldly life or spiritual truths,
etching it again and again upon their hearts.

동굴 벽화

동굴에 갇혀 사는 무리
어둠이 싫어 빛이 그리워
벽에 해와 달을 그리는지
낮에는 기차게 사냥하고
밤에는 서러워 눈물 흘리지

말 타고 활 쏘며 창 들어
배 채우려 자리 넓히려
짐승사냥 사람사냥
닥치는 대로 살육하지

쓰러뜨려 먹으려는 순간
헐떡이다 마지막 숨 내쉬는
형언 못 할 그 눈과 마주쳤지
그 안에 담긴 알 수 없는 세계

영혼 깊이 박힌 그 눈빛
두려우나 그 나라가 그리워
마음을 가다듬어 벽화를 그리지
세상살이와 영적일지
가슴판에 그리고 또 그리지

| Epilogue |

Circle

Starting from a single point,
I keep drawing a circle,
Its diameter endlessly expanding.

On the ground,
In the water,
In deep space,
On the horizon of the mind.

Though unseen,
Perhaps,
It rides the waves of eternity.

The circle once closed
Gradually opens and grows wider,
The earth spreads out beneath,
The sky draws closer.

The higher I rise,
The broader the circle expands,
Climbing ever higher, ever deeper.

| 에필로그 |

동그라미

한 점에서 시작해
한없이 지름이 커지는
동그라미를 그려 가지

땅에서
물에서
심우주에서
뇌의 지평에서

보이지는 않으나
아마도
영원의 파도를 타리

갇혔던 동그라미가
점점 열려 지면서
땅이 발아래로 깔려 가리
하늘이 더 가까이 다가오지

올라갈수록
넓어지는 동그라미
더 높이 깊이 기어오르지

About the Author
Lee Won-Ro

Poet as well as medical doctor (cardiologist), professor, chancellor of hospitals and university president, Lee Won-Ro's career has been prominent in his brilliant literary activities along with his extensive experiences and contributions in medical science and practice.

Lee Won-Ro is the author of sixty one poetry books along with fifteen anthologies. He also published extensively including ten books related to medicine both for professionals and general readership.

Lee Won-Ro's poetic world pursues the fundamental themes with profound aesthetic enthusiasm. His work combines wisdom and knowledge derived from his scientific background with his artistic power stemming from creative imagination and astute intuition.

Lee Won-Ro's verse embroiders refined tints and serene tones on the fabric of embellished words.

Poet Lee Won-Ro explores the universe in conjunction with his expertise in intellectual, affective and spiritual domains as a specialist in medicine and science to create his unique artistic world.

This book along with "Vertical and Horizontal", "That Day, That Moment", "The Sound of Waves", "Weather Vane", "Countdown", "On the Road", "Winter Gift", "Fair Winds", "Spiral Staircase", "The Watershed", "The Seed of Eternity", "Milky Way In DNA", "Signs of Recovery", "Applause", "Invitation", "Night Sky", "Revival", "The Promise", "Time Capsule", "The Tea Cup and the Sea", "The Tunnel of Waves", "The Tomorrow within Today, "Flowers and Stars", Corona Panic", "Chorus", "Waves", "Thanks and Empathy", "Red Berries, "Dialogue", "A Mural of Sounds", "Focal Point", "Day Break", "Prelude to a Pilgrimage", "Rehearsal", "TimeLapse Panorama", "Eve Celebration", "A Trumpet Call", "Right on Cue", "Why Do You Push My Back", "Space Walk", "Phoenix Parade", "The Vortex of Dances", "Pearling", "Priming Water", "A Glint of Light", "The River Unstoppable", "Song of Stars", "The Land of Floral Buds", "A Flute Player", "The Glow of a Firefly", "Resonance", "Wrinkles in Time", "Wedding Day", "Synapse". "Miracles are Everywhere", "Unity in Variety" and "Signal Hunter" are available at Amazon.com/author/leewonro or kdp.amazon.com/book shelf(paperbacks and e-books.

글쓴이
이원로

시인이자 의사(심장전문의), 교수, 명예의료원장, 전 대학교총장인 이원로 시인은 『월간문학』으로 등단, "빛과 소리를 넘어서", "햇빛 유난한 날에", "청진기와 망원경", "팬터마임", "피아니시모", "모자이크", "순간의 창", "바람의 지도", "우주의 배꼽", "시집가는 날", "시냅스", "기적은 어디에나", "화이부동", "신호추적자", "시간의 주름", "울림", "반딧불", "피리 부는 사람", "꽃눈 나라", "별들의 노래", "멈출 수 없는 강물", "섬광", "마중물", "진주 잡이", "춤의 소용돌이", "우주유영", "어찌 등을 미시나요", "불사조 행렬", "마침 좋은 때에", "나팔소리", "전야제", "타임랩스 파노라마", "장도의 서막", "새벽", "초점", "소리 벽화", "물결", "감사와 공감", "합창", "코로나 공황", "대화", "뻘간 열매", "꽃과 별", "바람 소리", "우리 집", "오늘 안의 내일", "파도의 터널", "찻잔과 바다", "타임 캡슐", "약속", "소생", "밤하늘", "초대장", "박수갈채", "회복의 눈빛", "DNA 안 은하수", "영원의 씨", "분수령", "나선 계단", "순풍", "겨울 선물", "길 위에서", "카운트다운", "바람개비", "파도소리", "그날 그때", "수직과 수평" 등 61권의 시집과 15권의 시선집을 출간했다. 그는 전공 분야의 교과서와 의학 정보를 일반인들에게 쉽게 전달하기 위한 실용서를 여러 권 집필했다.

이원로 시인의 시 세계에는 생명의 근원적 주제에 대한 탐색이 담겨져 있다. 그의 작품은 과학과 의학에서 유래된 지혜와 지식을 배경으로 기민한 통찰력과 상상력을 동원하여 진실하고 아름답고 영원한 우주를 추구하고 있다. 그의 시는 순화된 색조와 우아한 운율의 언어로 예술적 동경을 수놓아간다.

    이원로 시인은 과학과 의학 전문가로서의 지성적, 감성적, 영적 경험을 바탕으로 그의 독특한 예술 세계를 개척해가고 있다. 이 시집을 비롯하여 "수직과 수평", "파도소리", "바람개비", "카운트다운", "길 위에서", "겨울 선물", "순풍", "나선 계단", "수령", "영원의 씨", "DNA 안 은하수", "회복의 눈빛", "초대장", "밤하늘", "소생", "약속", "타임캡슐", "찻잔과 바다", "파도의 터널", "오늘 안의 내일", "우리집", "바람 소리", "꽃과 별", "빨간 열매", "파도의 터널", "우리집", "오늘 안의 내일", "바람 소리", "꽃과 별", "빨간 열매", "대화", "코로나 공황", "합창", "물결", "감사와 공감", "소리 벽화", "초점", "새벽", "장도의 서막", "타임랩스 파노라마", "전야제", "나팔소리", "마침 좋은 때에", "어찌 등을 미시나요", "우주유영", "불사조 행렬", "춤의 소용돌이", "진주잡이", "마중물", "섬광", "멈출 수 없는 강물", "별들의 노래", "꽃눈 나라", "피리 부는 사람", "반딧불", "울림", "시집가는 날", "시냅스", "기적은 어디에나", "화이부동", "신호 추적자", "시간의 주름" 등은 아래에서 구입할 수 있다. Amazon.com/author/leewonro와kdp.amazon.com/bookshelf(paperbacks and e-books)